Freshwater Turtles

Dr. Richard A. NeSmith

Love of Nature Series

ISSUE 11

FRESHWATER TURTLES

Many freshwater turtles are located in the southeastern United States, the world's highest concentration of turtle species, second only to southeastern Asia. Some North American turtles are doing well. Others are endangered or threatened. Some of the most populated freshwater turtles include softshell and flat shell turtles, mud and musk turtles, pond and box turtles, snapping turtles, and many more! Some species also have several sub-species.

The first step in understanding freshwater turtles (and sea turtles, too) is understanding what it means to be a ***reptile*** (meaning *creeping or crawling animal*). Reptiles are cold-blooded vertebrate animals. They breathe air with lungs and have skin made up of specialized dry scales or bony plates/scutes (or both). And, they lay leathery eggs on dry land. Reptiles include alligators, lizards, crocodiles, snakes, tortoises, and turtles.

Range

Turtles, like all reptiles, are cold-blooded or **ectotherms**. We will see that this concept is vitally important. Because of the ectotherm "lifestyle," the limiting factor for *where* freshwater turtles live is based on the climate or temperature. *Most reptiles* live only south of 40° North latitude, and almost no reptiles are found above 60° North. The United States and Canada border is at latitude 54.5° N (on the western coast) and 45° N (on the eastern coast). Temperatures above that latitude exceed most turtles' and other reptiles' physiological/biochemical limitations.

Characteristics

FRESHWATER TURTLES

How turtles monitor their body temperature is so vitally important that it requires an explanation. Reptiles, being cold-blooded animals, have a slower **metabolism** (called *bradymetabolism*). As a result, they possess **heat-seeking behaviors**. *You may recall that cold-blooded* does not describe whether they prefer or do not prefer cold or hot temperatures. Instead, it is *how* they maintain body heat.

There are two ways of describing **metabolism**: **endotherms** and **ectotherms**. Reptiles are ectotherms. *Ecto-* refers to external, as in outside the body. *Endo-* means within and relates to the inner or inside the body. Reptiles regulate body temperature by exchanging heat with their surrounding environment. Endotherms, like humans, create their body heat internally. So, turtles are ectotherms.

However, turtles have such erratic body temperature controls; they are given a unique name. They are referred to as **poikilotherms** (*poikilo* meaning varied). Therefore, they are both ectotherms and poikilotherms.

In comparison, mammals metabolize sugar in the liver, which provides heat to their body. Most of this **metabolism** occurs in the liver, and the heat is necessary to cause our enzymes to function correctly. Reptiles, however, produce very little heat. Instead, they regulate their temperature by moving into or out of the sunshine.

For turtles, this is a deficiently slow metabolism. So, they must regulate their heat by moving into and out of the sunshine. For turtles, if they become too warm, they must move back into the water. The water absorbs their body heat, lowering their temperature. Turtles need to sunbathe frequently to warm themselves and maintain their higher body temperatures.

Benefits of Cold-blooded

The benefit of being cold-blooded is that turtles do not have to feed as often as warm-blooded animals and can go for a long time between meals. This difference may seem like a poor trade-off. Reptiles can, however, survive on **10 percent *fewer*** calories required by similarly-sized endotherms.

Disadvantages of Cold-blooded

The disadvantage of being an ectotherm/poikilotherm is that the **enzymes** in their body do not adequately react except at a given temperature. So, enzymes are *temperature* *sensitive* to provide proper functioning of the muscles, digestion system, etc. Therefore, they will be very slow and sluggish in cold environments, such as early mornings. To function properly, they have to obtain the heat needed to activate enzymes. But, on the other hand, too much heat denatures[1] protein and enzymes and can kill the animal. It's a real see-saw event, explaining why turtles and other reptiles live in or near water. That is why they are also frequently in and out of the water to regulate body temperature.

As we will see in the discussion on reproduction, all reptiles, including aquatic ones, lay their eggs on land. So,

---

[1] Denaturing *destroys* proteins and they cannot be repaired. An example is an egg (albumin protein) being fried. It alters the protein permanently and renders it unable to function.

the relationship between land and water is a vital one. That is what partly determines where turtles can be found.

Freshwater turtles are *tetrapods* (four-legged). The scaly skin or scutes (plates) on turtles are made of sheets of a pliable but tough, waxy, lipid-like waterproof protein called *keratin*. This protein is the same from which hair and fingernails are made. This fibrous covering enables reptiles to live on land but cannot use their skin for breathing (cutaneous respiration), as do amphibians. So, all turtles breathe with lungs. However, a few turtles can obtain some oxygen from the water. This process can occur in two ways: ❶ through the skin (on their long necks) ❷ through an opening near their rear-end (called a *cloaca*). In addition, many turtles can completely retract their heads and feet into their shells.

Diet

Freshwater turtle diets are as varied as the number of species. Each species can have a very broad or very narrow type of diet. Some turtles are **omnivores** and eat meat, vegetation, or **carrion**. Some are strictly **herbivores** and eat just vegetation. Some turtles are opportunistic (passive hunters) and eat whatever they can find. Others are predatory and might chase or sit-in-wait (stealth) to catch their prey (active hunters). *Most turtles*, however, are omnivores, eating animals, plants, or carrion.

What a turtle eats depends on its species. More specifically, it depends on

❶ what kind of jaw it has for masticating (chewing) food

FRESHWATER TURTLES

❷ where it lives, and
❸ what food sources are available.

Most meals include worms, snails, aquatic insects, larvae, beetles, caterpillars, crustaceans, frogs, snakes, fish, and even other turtles or turtle eggs. Plant diets can consist of water plants, algae, fallen fruit, berries, mushrooms, flowers, and land plants grazed upon, such as grasses.

Behavior

Most basking turtles are ***diurnal*** (active during the day),

FRESHWATER TURTLES

such as those frequently seen basking in the sunshine.

Some, however, like the snapping turtle, are **nocturnal** and hunt at night. They lie in wait and dangle their tongue (*lingual lure*) with what appears to be a worm, hoping to lure fish to them. In cold weather, some reptiles, such as turtles, **brumate**. Brumation is similar to hibernation, for the animal becomes less active and can go for long periods without eating. It is not hibernation, however, because the reptiles are not asleep or living off fat reserves. Instead, their metabolism has slowed in response to the cold temperatures. The turtle becomes very sluggish. The amount of time in brumation is directly related to the low/cold environmental temperatures.

Often when a turtle is picked up off the ground, it will urinate (pee) on the person. They are frightened of being up off the ground and up in the air since that is not something they ever do. They can scratch a person with their clawed feet.

Understanding reptiles helps us to understand turtles, even with there being such a variety of species. Though generalizing most turtles, we will take a moment to briefly focus on three of the most common freshwater turtles in the US: the **red-eared sliders** (or terrapins), the **softshell** turtles, and the **snapping** turtles.

RED-EARED SLIDERS (Trachemys *scripta*)

FRESHWATER TURTLES

The red-eared slider is native to the Mississippi River. These turtles are also called **terrapins**, from an Algonquian Indian word meaning "a little turtle." They live in brackish, swampy water and drainages, lakes, freshwater rivers, or streams. They are a smaller subspecies to pond sliders, the common medium-sized semiaquatic turtles.

Though red-eared sliders are often mistaken as invasive species, they are **native** (**indigenous** or **endemic**) to the southern United States and northern Mexico. However, sliders have been popular in the pet trade. So, they have ended up in other local habitats where pet-owners released them. And many have been introduced to other parts of the world this way. Unfortunately, in doing so, they have become an invasive species to those areas.

The red-eared slider gets its name from the small red stripe or marking around its ears. It sort of looks like a racing stripe. And *slider* from its ability to slide quickly off rocks and logs into the water. One subspecies, the yellow-bellied slider, occurs naturally in north Florida. Red-eared sliders breed with yellow-bellied sliders there.

The **carapace** (shell) is a modified ribcage. It is divided into the dorsal (back) and the **plastron** (stomach or ventral side). The carapace of the red-eared slider can reach more than 16 inches (40 cm) in length. The average size ranges from 6 to 8 inches (15 to 20 cm) long. Females of the species are usually larger than the males. The term for different sizes or characteristics in males and females is *sexual dimorphism*.

The shell is oval and flattened, especially in the male. The color of the turtle shell changes depending on age and usually has a dark green background with light and dark variations and is covered in stripes and marking that seem to act as camouflage. Young sliders are leaf green and turn shades between brown and olive green.

Their life expectancy is shorter when in captivity, and they can live 20 to 30 years. Some individuals in the wild have lived for more than 40 years. The quality of their living environment has a strong influence on their lifespans and wellbeing.

FLORIDA SOFTSHELL TURTLES (Apalone *ferox*)

Softshell turtles, native to the southeastern United States, are **foragers** and prefer to submerge in mud when on land. The Florida softshell turtle is found primarily in Florida and the southern regions of South Carolina, Georgia, Alabama, Tennessee, and Texas. These turtles inhabit almost every freshwater habitat. They even tolerate some brackish environments. They prefer habitats with slow-moving or still water, including swamps, lakes, marshes, wet prairies, small rivers, creeks, and even human-made ponds, ditches, or sinkholes.

FRESHWATER TURTLES

They are vulnerable to predators due to their lack of a hard shell. However, softshell turtles can be very aggressive and can be dangerous. These turtles have extraordinarily long necks, powerful jaws, and clawed feet. Handling them is not advised.

Florida softshell turtles can live in the wild up to 50 years of age, but most live from 20-36 years. Though not threatened in the US, there is still some environmental pressure due to habitat destruction and pollution, notably chemical pollution, including prescription medications being flushed down toilets. These turtles are almost entirely aquatic.

Softshells only emerge from the water to bask or lay eggs. In the water, they prefer to bury themselves in the sandy/muddy bottom. Like all softshells, they are very fast-

FRESHWATER TURTLES

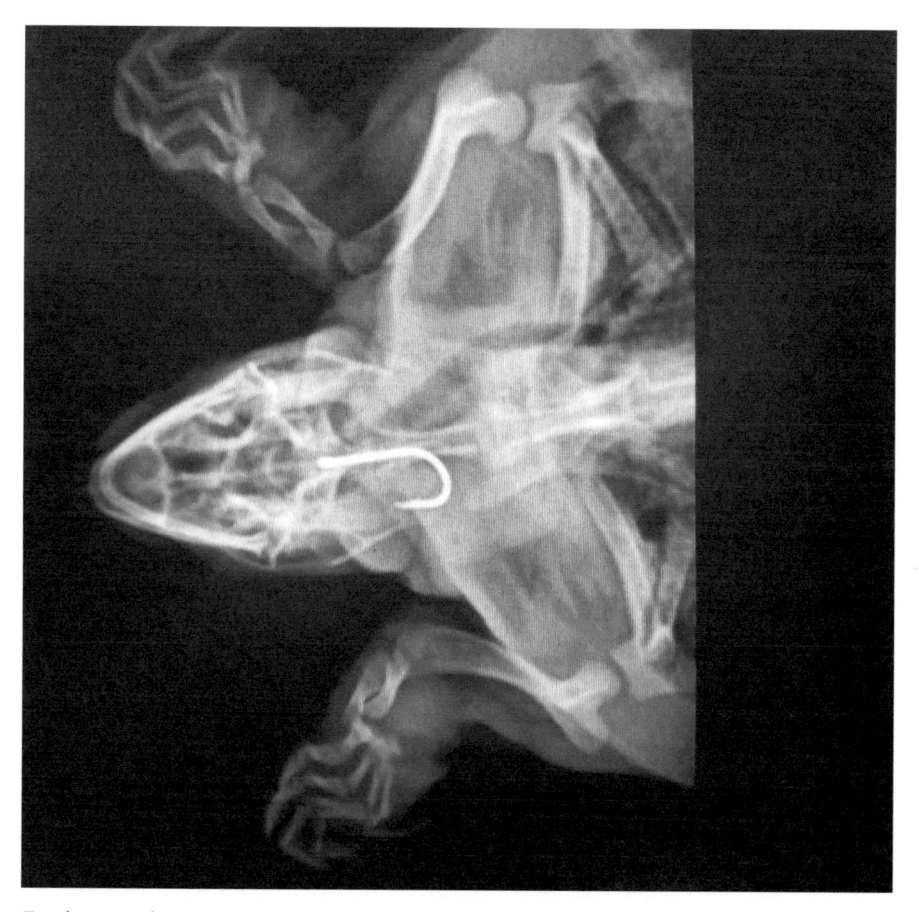

Turtle x-ray during Dr. Laurie's evaluation of a fishing hook removal.

webbed feet with three claws.[2] Their leathery carapace easily glides as it moves through water but is cumbersome on land. These turtles can remain active all year-round in warm areas of their range but become inactive during cold days. Some of these can brumate in the mud for four or more months at a time.

This turtle has a flattened, pancake-like body, a very long

---

[2] River terrapins have four front claws while painted terrapins have 5. Both have five hind claws.

neck, and an extended-looking head with a long snorkel-like nose or snout with two visible nostrils. The carapace is made of cartilaginous skin instead of **scutes**. Softshell turtles are olive-like green to dark brown and well camouflaged from most predators. Hatchlings are lighter in color and have yellow and orange markings with a rim around the shell. In addition, there are stripes on the face and neck. The plastron is usually darker in color. The colors fade as they age, generally becoming a dull, dark brown, concealing them well on muddy bottoms.

SNAPPING TURTLES (Chelydra *serpentine*)

The common snapping turtle is a large freshwater turtle with a range extending from southeastern Canada, southwest to the edge of the Rocky Mountains, and as far east as Nova Scotia and Florida. It is a cousin to the more massive alligator snapping turtle (Macrochelys *temminckii*), reaching up to 176 lbs. (79.8 kg).

These vigorous turtles have a vicious temperament and are noted for their aggressive nature out of the water. Though lacking body armor in comparison to other turtles, they make up for it in aggression. Their necks are incredibly long; thus, the species name *serpentine* (meaning snake-like). It can extend the long neck out unexpectedly fast to bite its confronter. With powerful jaws and razor-sharp beaks, it can easily penetrate the skin, break a bone, or remove a finger or two.

In water, they are highly mobile and generally flee and hide in underwater sediment. They are always scavenging and cleaning detritus (waste or debris) from the waters. A vast number of hatchlings do not make it to maturity. Juvenile snapping turtles are darker, nearly black, and tend to have a more wrinkled carapace than adults. Most freshwater turtles have such an effect on the environment they are considered *keystone species*. If they are removed, the ecosystem will change drastically.

Like most turtles, the snapping turtle brings in the biodiversity of flora and fauna with their presence. Also, they spread seeds that grow into plants that support fish nurseries and wetland ecosystems. In one example, 70% of fish and wildlife in Ontario relied upon snapping turtles to survive.

Though most snapping turtles are most vulnerable as eggs or hatchlings, they have fewer natural predators after reaching an ample size. Most who die beyond natural causes are hit by cars when crossing roads, searching for new ponds, or nesting sites. In captivity, they can live up to 47 years of age. In the wild, the lifespan is closer to 30 years.

One of the main physical characteristics of all snapping turtles is their unusually long tail. The tail often has a spiky ridge extending down its length, resembling that of a dinosaur. Like most aquatic turtles, male snapping turtles possess longer, thicker tails than females.

COOTER TURTLES (Pseudemys *concinna*)

There are many species of cooter turtles. They are native to the central and eastern United States. The name *cooter* is believed to have come from an African word "kuta," meaning "turtle" in the Bambara and Malinké languages. These turtles, it is thought, were brought to America by

FRESHWATER TURTLES

African slaves. Though the cooter can be found in ponds and lakes, they prefer slow-moving streams and creeks.

One of the unique features of a cooter turtle is breathing through a process called *cloacal respiration*. Water pumps through its back end (cloaca) into a cloacal sac where it is exposed to long thread-like fibers that remove oxygen from the water through diffusion. This form of gas exchange is simply the diffusion of oxygen in and carbon dioxide out. This exchange enables the cooter to stay underwater for extended periods. Though turtles, in general, can hold their breath for a very long time, they all have to come up to breathe every so often, or they will drown.

PAINTED TURTLES (Chrysemys *picta*)

Painted turtles and their numerous subspecies are the most widespread native turtle of North America. They have bright yellowish lines and greenish skin on their body. Or they may have yellow with reddish stripes running from the face back to the body. They live in slow-moving freshwater, from southern Canada to northern Mexico and from the Atlantic to the Pacific. They prefer ponds and lakes. This species is often confused with the cooter turtles. These seem to be the most popular type of turtle pet.

Painted turtles tend to stay smaller than most turtles, growing to be between four and 12 inches long (10.2-30.5 cm), with **sexual dimorphism** (the males being smaller than the females). They are omnivorous and often seen basking on logs or upon rocks. These turtles, and a few others, tend to climb up on one another while basking (*stacking*). Remembering how vital the sun's rays are for

temperature regulation, turtles pile on top of each other to get exposed to more sun-rays.

With stacking, it is believed that the turtles are not

FRESHWATER TURTLES

struggling to get on top of each other. Instead, they are trying to position themselves underneath one another. Too much heat and they can die quickly. Back and forth into the water (or shade) and back up on the rocks is a daily, sometimes hourly routine. At night, the turtle returns to the bottom of the lake or pond and sleeps. Finally, the turtle will bury itself in the pond mud or on a nearby muddy short in cold regions, entering brumation.

Reproduction

All turtles are *ovoviviparous* (lay eggs). They seek a place on

Turtles make fast tracks in their escape.

land to lay their eggs, upon which finding a suitable location, dig a hole in the ground as a nest in the sand or dirt, then leave it behind. No species of turtle provides care or nurturing of their young. Mating age depends on the species of the turtle. And some mate within a few years and others require 50 years to mature. Some species battle others for the right to mate, and others are quick to mate with a mating ritual.

Mating is somewhat acrobatic. Turtles must arrange their bodies in such a way as to open and separate the back shell of both turtles, with their tails in perfect alignment. The number of eggs laid also depends on species, with some laying two or three eggs and others laying 100 or more into the nest. Like alligators, the temperature of the nest (sand) is critical in determining the sex of the babies (hatchling). The "perfect" climate produces an even amount of male and female offspring. Higher temperatures make females. Turtles can slide, glide, walk, and swim within hours of birth.

Female snapping turtles travel overland in search of sandy soil. The female will dig a hole, lay her clutch of eggs (25 to 80 each year), and guide the eggs into the nest using her hind legs. If disturbed, she will stop after laying an egg and then move on. This strategy often engages the predator's attention on the laid egg long enough for the female to find a more secluded location. When finished, she covers the eggs with the sand and leaves with no maternal duty. The sun's heat incubates and protects the eggs unless some predator like a raccoon or crow comes along and digs them up.

The chance of hatching depends on whether the nest is found out. New hatchlings (about the size of a US quarter) face all kinds of risks and perils before reaching adulthood. The journey from nest to water is tense with danger. Birds, raccoons, opossums, weasel, skunks, and baby alligators all prey on young turtles. Until a turtle reaches a larger size, it will be vulnerable. For many species, only about 1 out of 160 hatchlings will make it to maturity. For some more unfortunate species, only 1 out of 1000 survive to adulthood. Ensuring a species' survival requires a proliferation of far more eggs to be laid so that some will hatch.

Miscellaneous

Though turtles do not have ears, they are not deaf. They do not have an outer ear, but they have thin flaps of skin (tympanum) covering internal ear bones. This flap receives vibrations and low-frequency sounds in the inner ear canal. Turtles can detect vibrations and even air movement, such as the wing-flapping of a bird, which aids in sensing prey or predator's presence. Hearing is useful underwater as well.

However, turtles tend to rely more upon their sense of vision and smell, both of which are well-developed.

© Phil Stone

Though the skin of a turtle is leathery, it is still very sensitive to touch. So is the shell. The skeleton (spine) fuses with the carapace. There are nerves in the carapace that enable the turtle to feel and know when something is touching its shell. So, they are sensitive to touch *and* pressure. Some with pet turtles have shared how their turtle enjoys a back rub. Some turtles also have taste buds, and some do not.

While we are out swimming, it may be tempting to want to catch a freshwater turtle. However, some states restrict this, and violators can be charged with harassing wildlife.

Various states have laws and regulations about capturing or possessing turtles. Some restrict access to them during breeding or egg-laying periods. In most cases, those wanting to capture and study turtles must secure a special permit to do so. In one local community, a lady was arrested for having a protected freshwater turtle in her truck's bed due to it being *out of season*.

Turtles can be disease-carrying. They can carry salmonella and various respiratory infections. These diseases are caused by bacteria transmitted to people. Also, turtles are subject to *shell rot*, which is an infection of their carapace. It is always good to carefully wash one's hands after handling an animal, and turtles are no exception.

Turtles are fascinating creatures. They play a vital and essential role in a healthy and vibrant aquatic community. Some people have enjoyed these animals as pets. They are fun to watch, and if out on the lake or river, you can watch them slip away into the water if you are quiet, quick, and look well ahead before approaching them.

REVIEW

1. How many species of turtles are found in the world?

2. How many of the world's turtle species are found in the US?

3. Explain how turtle survives during the cold winters?

4. How is the red-eared slider different from the common snapping turtle?

5. Which turtle discussed was your favorite? Why did you select that species?

6. What is brumation, and what does it have to do with turtles?

7. Which turtle grows the largest? Why would you not want to fight with it?

8. You decided on a class project to capture a few turtles to study for a report. What do you need to do before you start?

9. What are the chances of a turtle hatchling surviving to adult?

10. Which turtle discussed would be the most likely pet?

FRESHWATER TURTLES

FRESHWATER TURTLES

ALLIGATOR SNAPPING TURTLE

COLORING PAGE

http://www.supercoloring.com/coloring-pages/walking-alligator-snapping-turtle

FRESHWATER TURTLES

Freshwater Turtles

Name:_____

Carefully read each statement or clue, then record the correct letters in the boxes provided. Use the word bank if necessary.

terrapins   brumate   liver   omnivore   darkens   cartilaginous   tetrapod   carapace

poikilotherm   reptile   ectotherm   keystone   Antarctica   bradymetabolism

Across
1. Four-legged
2. Means creeping or crawling animal
3. For mammals, where does our body heat come from?
5. Turtles are very adaptive and can be found on every continent except _____.
7. Often as a turtle grows older its shell color ____.
10. Body of softshell turtles is?
11. Term for 'shell.'
12. Regulates body temperature externally
13. Remove this type of animal or species and the environment changes greatly.

Down
1. Another name for slider turtles
4. Means slow body metabolism
6. Name given if body temperature is really erratic.
8. Diet consist of meats and plants
9. For of resting during cold weather that slows down body metabolism

37

FRESHWATER TURTLES

INTERESTING SOURCES TO CONSIDER

Alligator, Turtles and Fish, Florida Keys Freshwater Pond. Available at: https://youtu.be/7jCVFHQtYIc

American Water Turtles. Old Book Illustrations. Available at: https://www.oldbookillustrations.com/illustrations/american-water-turtles/

BITTEN by a SNAPPING TURTLE! Brave Wilderness. Available at: https://youtu.be/F57z6ya-rnA

Catching Huge Snapping Turtles at Night. Available at: https://youtu.be/APyNDdvfXso

Florida Soft Shell Turtle. Available at: https://youtu.be/auEoqNPialI

Florida Trappers Catch New Species Of Monster-Sized Suwannee Alligator Snapping Turtles. Available at: https://youtu.be/YCdO1WK3Ew8

Freshwater Turtles of North America. Available at: https://www.pinterest.com/pin/474637248222027282/

Softshell Turtle facts: The largest living freshwater turtles. Animal Fact Files. Available at: https://youtu.be/LNNoqXQMH_4

Tracking Spotted Turtles in Florida. Available at: https://youtu.be/ioa2X0wLIzA

Turtle of North America. Available at: https://www.inaturalist.org/guides/2092

Turtle vs Tortoise. National Geographic: BBC Documentary. Available at: https://www.youtube.com/watch?v=VoiGsRcCZBg

Turtles Breathe out of their Butts. McGill University Office of Science and Society. Available at: https://www.mcgill.ca/oss/article/did-you-know/turtles-breathe-out-their-butt

Turtles of North American. Available at: https://www.inaturalist.org/guides/2092

US Fish and Wildlife Services. International Affairs. Available at: https://www.fws.gov/international/animals/freshwater-turtles.html

FRESHWATER TURTLES

Above: *Close up of the claw of a large alligator snapping turtle.* **Below:** *Clutch of eggs dug up from nest and feasted upon by a predator raccoon or opossum.*

Many small turtles are preyed upon by alligators.

ABOUT THE AUTHOR

Richard NeSmith is a native of Florida, USA. He grew up wading through the swamps of central Florida with his two younger brothers during the pre-Disney era, and unknowingly, falling in love with biology, wildlife, and nature. He has lived in seven American states, twice in Australia and once in Mexico City. He holds eight university degrees and has taught for 14 years in secondary schools, here and abroad, and another 13 years as a professor in several American universities. His service includes professor of science education, Dean of Education, Campus Dean, as well as an online instructor. His passion for learning (and *how we learn*) did not develop until *after* graduating from high school. His only explanation for this is that *having a goal made all the difference in the world*. He enjoys reading, hiking, nature photography, golf, and tennis.

http://richardnesmith.obior.cc

FRESHWATER TURTLES

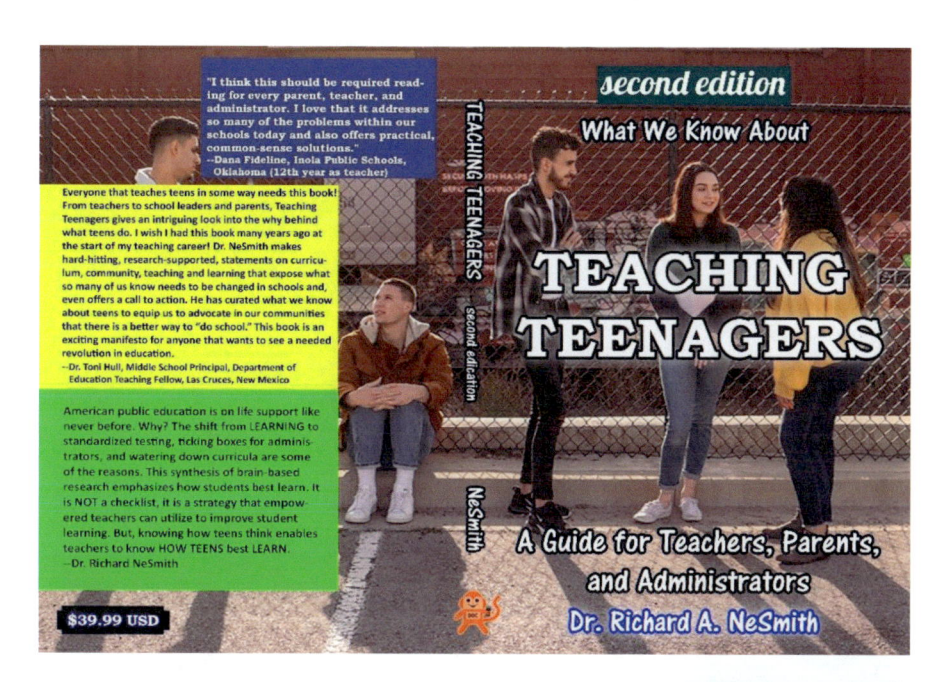

Applied Principles of Education & Learning
presents

APE-Learning

AMAZON AUTHOR's PAGE:
https://www.amazon.com/author/richardnesmith

Educational, wildlife, and naturalist books available by Dr. Richard NeSmith

FACEBOOK: https://bit.ly/3a9RSrf

YouTUBE: https://bit.ly/3mq8j8w

41

FRESHWATER TURTLES

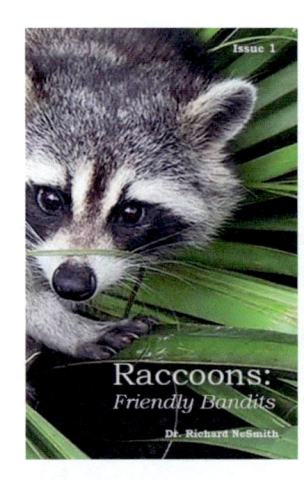

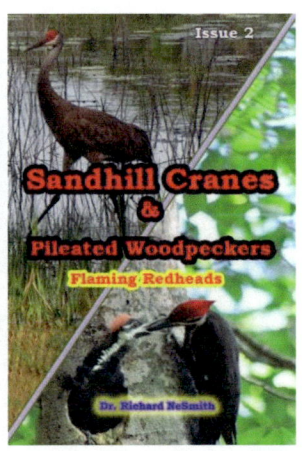

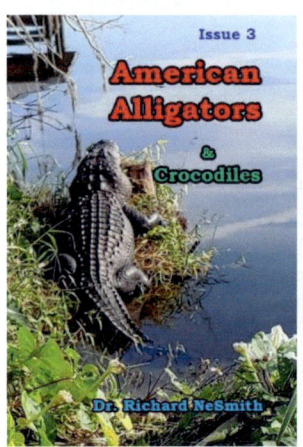

FRESHWATER TURTLES

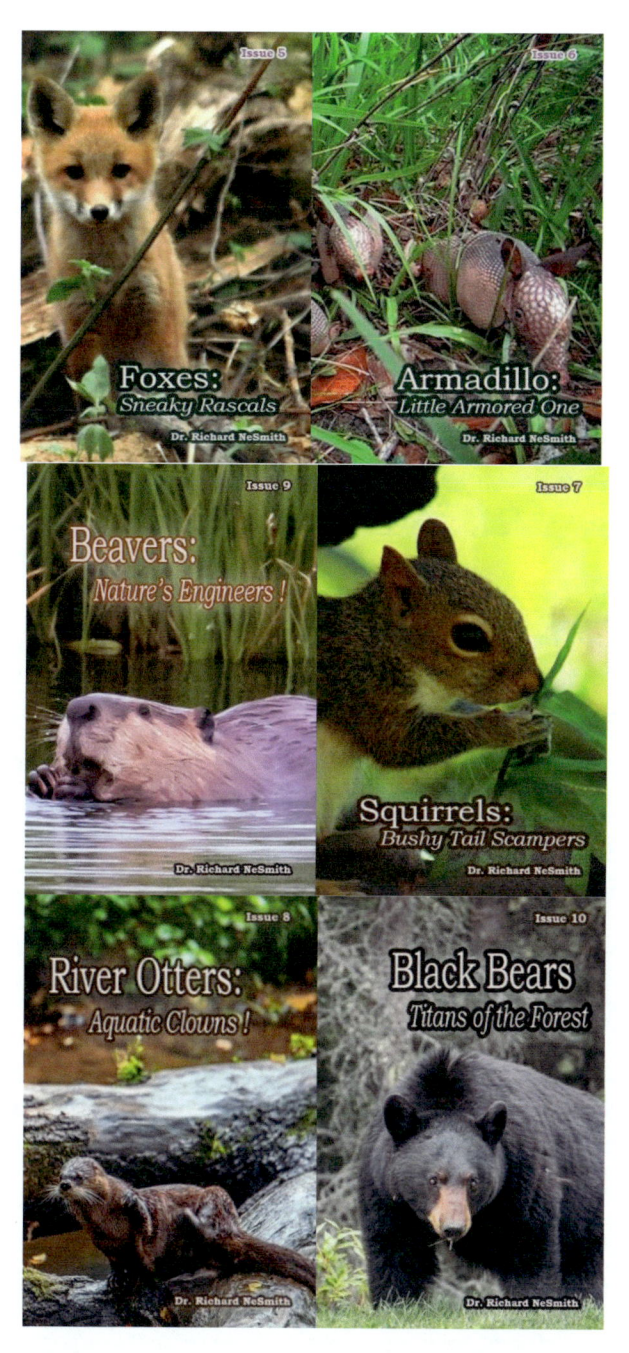

Issue 5 — Foxes: Sneaky Rascals — Dr. Richard NeSmith

Issue 6 — Armadillo: Little Armored One — Dr. Richard NeSmith

Issue 9 — Beavers: Nature's Engineers! — Dr. Richard NeSmith

Issue 7 — Squirrels: Bushy Tail Scampers — Dr. Richard NeSmith

Issue 8 — River Otters: Aquatic Clowns! — Dr. Richard NeSmith

Issue 10 — Black Bears: Titans of the Forest — Dr. Richard NeSmith

http://amazon.com/author/richardnesmith

FRESHWATER TURTLES

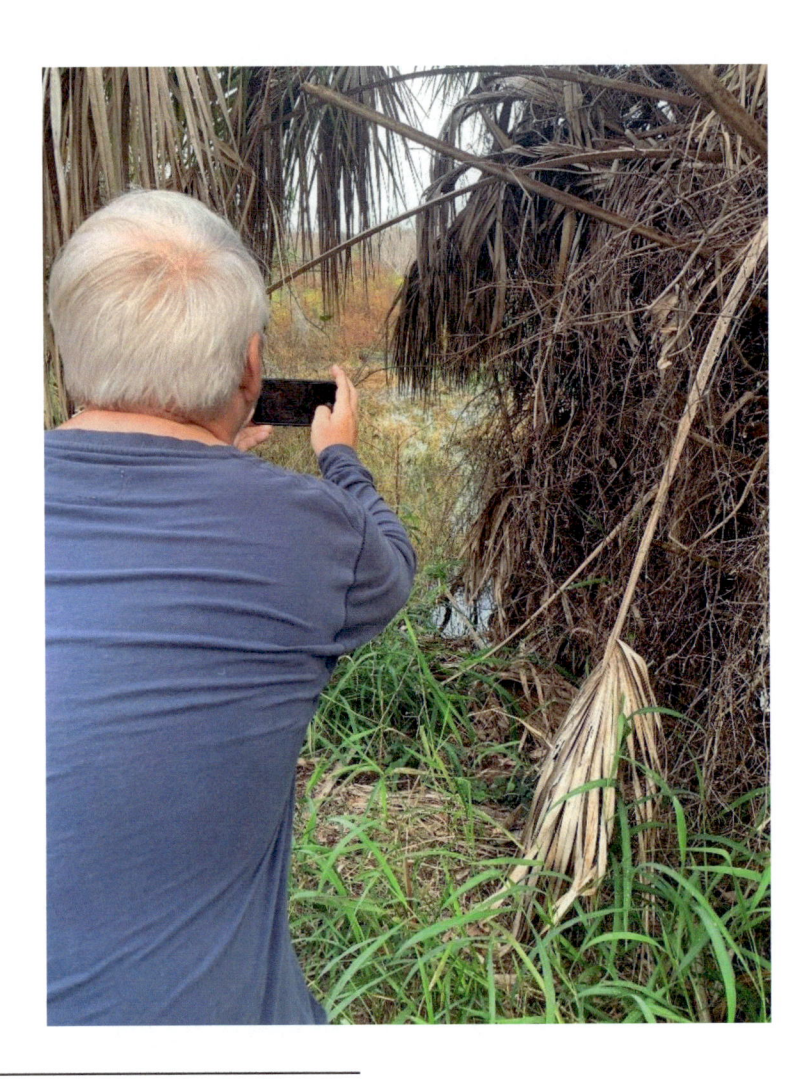

[i] Special thanks to the following who kindly provided permission to use their photographs on pixaby.com (Erika Ledoux, nataniel67, Scottslm, zoosnow, and vujicivana).

Thank you to Jonathon Kemp and Feft9mrnxV0on from Unsplash.

In addition, special thanks to **Cindy Frasier, Stacey Diamond, Randy Johnson, Greg Jowers, Phil Stones,** and **Karen Devins**. And, as always, special thanks to **Dr. Laurie Aleixo**, for her relief work, her photographs (and x-ray of the hook removal), and her support and encouragement. ***Thank you all.***

Made in United States
Troutdale, OR
04/14/2025